Silver Box

poems by

Natachee Momaday Gray

Finishing Line Press
Georgetown, Kentucky

There are those who believe that the earth is dead. They are deceived. The earth is alive, and it is possessed of spirit. Consider the holy tree. It can be allowed to thirst. It can be cut down. Worst of all, it can be denied our faith in it, our belief. But if we speak to it, if we pray, it will thrive.

—N. Scott Momaday

Silver Box

For My Family

Copyright © 2023 by Natachee Momaday Gray
ISBN 979-8-88838-142-7 First Edition
All rights reserved under International and Pan-American Copyright Conventions. No part of this book may be reproduced in any manner whatsoever without written permission from the publisher, except in the case of brief quotations embodied in critical articles and reviews.

ACKNOWLEDGMENTS

I'm grateful to the following publications in which some of these poems first appeared:

Taos Journal of International Poetry and Art: "Silver Box"
(RE) An Ideas Journal: "Honey Black"

I'm also grateful to the following venues in which several poems in this collection were featured in the spoken word:

Teatro Paraguas, Santa Fe, New Mexico
The Richard Eeds Radio Show, Santa Fe, New Mexico
Collected Works Bookstore, Santa Fe, New Mexico
The Harwood Museum (SOMOS reader), Taos, New Mexico

Publisher: Leah Huete de Maines
Editor: Christen Kincaid
Cover Art: Catherine Schroeder
Author Photo: Brandon Soder
Cover Design: Elizabeth Maines McCleavy

Order online: www.finishinglinepress.com
also available on amazon.com

Author inquiries and mail orders:
Finishing Line Press
PO Box 1626
Georgetown, Kentucky 40324
USA

Table of Contents

Silver Box 1

After Tulips Die 2

Blood's Burden 5

Anything for Billy 7

Caelsha 9

Cinéma 11

Common Mallow 15

Flores y Comida 16

Honey Black 18

Love 21

Sancocho 23

Twenty Five 25

Nevada 26

Muerte 31

With Thanks 33

Silver Box

I've written so fondly of heaven,
so many times.
The egg white,
the ruffle over breast,
how rugged the soil for garlic.

The tin square is an opening to heaven.
Galisteo etching,
place for worship.
Dry heave, splinter, caress.
Blood in the sheets.
Rinds of bright red melon.
And why are you so far away from me now?
Remember when I sat on your lap,
and you struggled to hold my weight?
Not because of my heaviness,
but precisely because of my fluidity and wetness,
and because I move so slowly.

Once, I held a tiny glass of dark blackberry port
in the archway of a gallery museum next to Jesus.
The last time I saw the gothic bay.
It transformed liquid to blood water
the last time I was by myself in a quiet room.

I feel raw in the small of my back,
skinned and fresh.
I'm a baby animal
birthed from water,
rain,
stem cells,
maritime trade.
There is a bartering systematic friction within the pulse.
Found teeth,
found roses,
strung with corn on the rosary.

After Tulips Die

Ripe heat shows its orange cranium,
a gut of misshape feigns an encampment
in the blood-pulp life pool along the way.
I was a child,
I am a child.
I let it smolder to an overcast amber,
to a hot honey consommé.
Pour it into a molding over toasted lilac esker.
To the rind where the ryegrass spreads.

I like the caramel against the black.
I like my rose ink to steep the plums.
We used to fatten our flourish by selling our tablature.
Music on paper, problem boy blues.
They were on the brink of hunger.
There became a new dispassionateness.
They had identical socks, checkered and stained,
and they were bald because they were in mourning.

I often think
if I were to sleep next to the water,
at the mystic back of the ocean,
would I see things that haven't been seen before?
Would ghost-holy silver fins and ribs still be impossible
if I were alone by the seashore
in the rondure of moon morning?

I haven't used my shelter
or seen the dog from my surgery dreams
since I was boy-like.
I am drawing again those abstractions
that I did as an infant artist,
as clear and as profound as they were then.

The destitute are the pumpkin tendrils.
They were the wagon-born tulip bulbs,
expecting to seed,
never dug up—
thick bruised lamb's ear,
pierced to dry in a lonely moment
dropped somewhere on the wilderness

of the White Angel breadline.
Pork knuckles sometimes.
One root mash, skin on, full belly reverie,
greenish handle glass pint of cold milk with its full fat.
Irrational female.
Hot light.
Velvet renegade.
Artichoke and cabbage.
A germinal lifeline that doesn't quite reach the wrist.

The road west externalizes a licorice partnership
with somebody's help and withdrawal.
I am proud to say that we looked like outlaws,
and we sang like them too.
"Billy, doesn't that gun make you feel weighted, Billy?"

White nudes on balconies,
daguerreotype,
the first snowfall captured in a still
do not compare to the beauty of your rag wrapped feet.
Rag wrapped ravens in the street.
A shoemaker's iron shapes the leather over the toe box.
Fix your erupting gaze on the momentous herding,
the cattle in the star box,
and walk the other way.

After tulips die, the leaves can be kept and crumbled.
After my tulips die, I am surrounded by the soul of them.
The wind offers graciousness and humility
but raptures with voluptuous barbarity.
My hands, I can see, are small and sodden.
When I pick the flowers now,
the dirt cherishes my fingers.
I love the winter bouquet more than the spring's.
It is an end rather than a beginning.
But there are lingering blooms
that hold on through the harshest of winter months
and are redolent in color and perfume.

In an inevitable January,
when my hands are different,

maybe the soil will not cherish the way it used to.
But I'll save the leaves anyway.
To be kept and crumbled,
to be curled in my hands when I leave.

I like my rose ink to steep the plums.
Irrational female.
Velvet renegade.
My germinal lifeline doesn't quite reach my wrist.

I was a child, and I am a child.
I fear and relish in that I will always be a child.
I draw with my eyes the abstractions that my father kept.

The mystic back of the ocean is similar
to the wagon-born tulips on the road West
to carouse with outlaws.
It's different drinking from a greenish handle glass pint
of cold milk with its full fat in the summertime
than it was in the winter nights with honey and warmth.

I pour the hot honey lilac over the veteran esker,
and I'll have the dog dream from my surgery year one last time.
The ghost-holy ancient silver fins and ribs
will show themselves in secret
when I'm alone by the seashore
in the rondure of moon morning.

Ripe heat shows its orange cranium
and a gut of misshape feigns an encampment
in the blood-pulp life pool along the way.

It ends,
with the lifeline,
molded over toasted lilacs,
seeping all the way to the rind where the ryegrass spreads.

The place that is blown past recollection,
into the bygone water,
to the caramel against the black,
to lay upon the story that continues after the tulips die.

Blood's Burden

In our house
rubicund blooms hang uprooted
without cloudburst in their verdant youth
in preservation of their green.
Their beauty is cradled in their babyhood.
Flower vitality drips
like lives out of velvet vegetable pores
into the unknown
and curls into a wet heaven
that is of the dirt instead of clouds.
Its essence, its very lasting perfume recollection,
remains,
drifting in the house.

The air stays immersed in a clean beige light
that is reminiscent of the petiole's spirit:
familial spirituality and my earliest dream memories
of ghosts in the north,
devotion to warmth, earnestness,
prayer, and wood in pieces,
scattered across the clay.
The earth, when I found it, was spread over lustrous prairie
before birth
existing in children,
to be listened to and haunted by.

Children created language after all.

He who is of the blood origin of bears
is gnostic in his extraction of words,
ever profound and bright.
Ancient and sedentary on the wind-gates of a realm
close to heart, blood foundation,
sitting atop human bristles in the bulk of daylight.
Exactly as a lion is.

At the foot-hilt of graves, always muted,
and always sojourned.
Protected under stone, visited in life,
and in dreams.

If blood were a place it would be settled and sewn with herbs.
Chamomile budding,
moths carried on the backs of wild horses.
If blood were an instance,
it would be saturated and enlightened.
Buckskin and water.

He articulates a romance of bygone time,
holding history in his breath.
Keeping ancestors from bleeding out of mind and memory.
He said that when his father was a boy,
he became a witness to the sunrise
as the dragonfly always is.
His story is without end, wetting the corners of lives,
creating acquaintance like rubicund blooms,
preserving the green in the words of the bear,
traveling alongside the language that children made.
His voice is mine.

As I visit the sun in its protrusion,
I stand in beige light
in a lustrous prairie,
with ghosts from the north
muted like graves,
heaven in the ground.
I speak his colloquy
in his voice that carries
in the language of my blood.
And I realize,
I too have been changed by his words.

Anything for Billy

I'm almost able to marry.
I see him between morning hours
in the yellow of the day.
Riding!
Half dead, half wounded,
amongst big, friendly spotted creatures.
A boy, freshly Twenty-One,
with liquor mud and marmalade blood
caked defiant on his boots.
Bumping along the horse-brown thigh of his best friend.

Both of them, buck tooth smiling,
riding frivolous
riding knowing,
riding uncaring
in my country.

He has matted chocolate curls.
Manhattan boy, my Lincoln cowboy,
coming to marry this Indian girl.

His gun, tucked away, always dangerous
in the canvas of his underclothes.

Petticoat armored,
dainty waist,
dainty wristed subjects swoon
and open their heavy doors to his please and thank you.

For Billy doesn't smoke tobacco anymore.

The time we spent in Lincoln was cradled in his belly
after he took those daring mouthfuls of the soft, rich candy.
It was the nectar of the land.

The memory of us as children,
scabbed, old blood mixing, carved in the pulp of his heart.

I wore a blue dress with white lace.
But then I took it off.

I left them rumpled in the washroom,
and replaced them with jeans and boots.

For Billy didn't go to church anymore.

It was a lovely ceremony,
and we lived, unkempt and vibrant young,
in a house that we built ourselves.

Before his death, we laughed a hundred times each day
and received light from that same yellow of the same day
when I last saw him.

I'm almost able to marry,
but I already have.

I always think of the time we spent together in Lincoln,
and the chestnut-bitter, marmalade-sweet
promise
between me and The Kid.

Caelsha

Always sweet one, ever and ever.
Familial gifts are small scarlet protrusions that bud
out of the thickness of cherry wood
and red bone marrow.
The scent of the ascending gardens is muffled
by the silver wind barrier.
Shall we wish for it to burst open to a sunny heart of daybreak
in a cornflower heaven?
Where we can smell the green stems of your favorite flowers
and the heat from around the earth?
Or shall I hold onto you forever,
your hands in mine,
your magnificent soul layered atop my own?

All I have ever wished a precious unfathomable being to attain
is painless love.
But somehow I carry with me the inherited subtle tinge
of butterfly ache
in the innermost pulp of my heart,
as you did long before I came into this world.

The open wounds are covered with lilacs.
We planted them together to seed by a certain organic time
within the span of a single rosy dawn.
Hundreds of fragrant, nostalgic buds will see their first sacred morning,
under the fading blue of the night before.
Everything that surrounds you will begin to attain your alexandrite.
You gave me so many cherished things.
A note with a picture of a sprouting tree that said,
"There are two gifts we can give to our children.
One is roots and the other is wings."

As a little girl I journeyed in my dreams
to the place where people had wings.
And I recognize the silky pearl sheen of yours now.
Mine are within, and I'll be able to use them sometimes,
so we can fly together.

You told me to be the voice in the wilderness,
because it is who I am.
I have cut down the twisting wiry shrubs

to make room for a little peaceful home for my heart,
surrounded by lilacs.
They are the livelihood and the comfort
from which our psyches were born.
Guarded by grandmother spider,
her soot and her babies.
Familial gifts are small scarlet protrusions
that bud from wood and marrow.
The roots become the wings,
like the seeds become the bloom,
like our ancestors become our legacy,
and a note becomes a relic.
I will hold your roots forever.
And you are blessed with wings.
Thank you for the gift.
Be the voice in the wilderness,
because it is who you are.
You speak,
and I will listen.

Cinéma

A remembrance strawberry cake
is cut into eighths to feed a memory of gliding ducks
in peach-boiled afternoons.
It will melt to a bluish cream to even coat the bellies of men
who are still derivatives of roasted corners at Minsky's.

Lower East Side Nickelodeon,
five cents for admission,
bare walls and hard seats.

One can still see the embossed cornice moldings on the corinthian columns,
and the engraved name on the north wing of The Gotham Theater in Harlem.

Theaters weren't air conditioned.
They were hot and lacking color on the inside.

He kept a chorus line and a band.
His hands were wet and green from brass.

Cinéma holds Nostalgia in its gaps.
The morning was damp at five and dry by noon,
and there was jazz at nine-thirty.

Something's missing.
More cake, some tools.

I'm shivering in my dressing room.
In the steps of the storage ladders
there is a remindful coruscation
of lavender sheep's milk and friend affection.

All of our wedding plates fell off the shelf once we hit our mark.
A warm bloom of trumpet and a lasting evergreen gusto
neutralize an otherwise prevented grin at lunchtime.
There are ones who are accustomed to illegitimate and intimate conversations
that take the space of an entire afternoon,
while there is neither food nor drink.

The hardened male figures on the covers of records from 1947
all have on little hats that are attractive in size because of the lighting.
I would have bought one for my children in the past.
Parents are piggy backing and hearty.

I was twenty.
I was in a dream state.
I wore overalls for the convenience of pockets.
I had outgrown many good writers.

It's sad too, the good ones were always blind.
Cinéma takes residence in hotels that host the overflow.
There is music in the marbles, Park Avenue Petite.
It doesn't consume.
It doesn't hang on.
It just spouts.

When I was eleven, I dreamt into the classroom,
and there was light on his face from the open window.
And I fell in love.
I wouldn't go to sleep.
There was too much to speak of, and too many spiders.

Sad times were celebrated violence,
and breath was even and fair.
Moroseness wasn't a covert sliver of a cheerful disposition.
He is light and lovely,

and he has sentiment for daffodils and distraction as I do.
I cannot bear an absence.
I love Porgy and I love postponement.
Certain infatuation is similar to subtle fondness and fasting.

Streets are companionless.
Two sisters walk into a cafe that is empty.
It smells of room temperature butter and teary grass.
I remember running through milky vision
in a warm wet garden before I was here.
People are freshly waking,
but sisters have been up for hours,
truck stop bumming and flying.

Opalescent Rose is her shade.
Mrs. Rubenstein's hefty samples were sold
next to bourgeois "Evening in Paris" compacts.
"We regret owing to wartime restrictions, PUFFS are unobtainable."
It was etched into the mirrors of the piano shaped disks.
Hitler hated makeup.

Cinéma is the scent that she carries.
Yves Saint Laurent created it for her.
I was wearing the same lipstick that she had on.
We shared it for most of our lives.
And the scent she let me borrow in my youth.
Its overture is a startling fragrance.
Glamorous.
White musk that fades into depth and mystery.
Its sentience batter is thick and ruby
like the mountain glitter from our sunbaths.

Temples are immersed in purple flowers like Twiggy's were.
Cinéma is close to my mother,
adhered to Nostalgia in one instance.

There is discoloration on the collarbone,
a strange patch of vinegar yellow.
The clang of church bells is mannish
and infecting and distracting.

It echoes always
and triggers an acute knowing.
A place of interest for chickens and humans,
as the grittiness of a silver screen is.

Cinéma is the closest occurrence to Nostalgia,
condensed.
An ashy complexion is not a bad one,
as long as you can hear the birds outside.

I cannot bear an absence.
It was he and she who first created a ribbon psychology in my life.
Two who I am in love with culturally,

unforgettably,
cinematically.
Like when Coco Chanel received her first sewing kit.
It'll be similar to dying.

For those who love first editions,
there are Sunday soirees in some arenas.
I miss being my Mama's baby,
and the squash blossoms and the buttercups.

The baby blue '65 bug is starting to disintegrate in the brackish water
somewhere along the coast.
My dressing table is marked with photographs,
and the sofa is dressed in my gowns.

Cinéma is close to Nostalgia.
Teeth stained from coffee,
hands green from brass.
I discovered later in my life,
when his arms draped around me,
his wrists were Baudelaire's.

Common Mallow

How often do purple flowers bloom
Against the scrim of neighboring umbrage?
The blackness,
As it is cast by trees,
Was formerly the grit of the renaissance window,
Spattering dusk onto the table with the asters.
A verdin is eating the New World spindles
From the tousled shrub,
Stretching mangled,
From old age,
Along the flank of blue swill.
They are forewarned by the blood on the honeysuckle.
The seeds eaten by larvae.
The horizon is ravaged by flies.

Once there was a farmland here:
A presence of linen hanging on clothespins,
The feeling of hominal belonging,
A lover's waltz into memory and into ashes,
A roll of brown posies wishing to burn toward heaven.

Once the tobacco fields are ready to harvest,
There will be no more waiting.
The job will have been completed,
And the flies will be gone.

The dress of double cotton
Is arrested in the breath,
Loosened by wind,
Stained from days of play
In the sky's turbid, fathomless hymn.
It awaits its landing atop the three lobed mericarp,
Cold from evening rain.

The core misses the sallow kerchief.
All around there are wisps of hollow wind.

I imagine myself sitting across from the one I cherish,
On our blue wooden chair,
In the garden of common mallow.
Known for its renowned draught tolerance,
The life blood in the memoir.

Flores y Comida

Cuanto vale el amor?
I feel like Venus today
and cupid tomorrow.

I love flowers,
and I love steak.
I love food with flowers,
and I love the prayer before a meal.
I like bloody, bloody steak,
the rarest you can make,
because I am rare.
Cut with the precision
of an elephantine mandolin
with many sides.

I am celebrating and enjoying living
in the avoirdupois of writing
my Poemas Sobre Mi Cuerpo.
Same as I am content
in writing my Poemas Sobre el Mar:
vast and sensuous and portly.

Cuanto vale dormir?
Soy raro y exquisito en mi cama contigo,
served with flowers on the horizontal pillows.
If Bartolomeo Scappi wanted to cook me—
make a rue from my bones in the 16th century,
simmer me with garlic and wine,
dust Italian roses—
I wouldn't question it.
I would enjoy it.

Cuanto vale la carne?
My brain is too runny like a bloody egg
devoured by summer.
Que recuerda a las bayas rojas?
A sky so glaringly amarillo y crema,
disfruto siendo,
un bebé,
covered in your fur,
taxidermy butterscotch.

Tu carne es marrón del sol,
and mine,
violet from the frost,
cauterized by my soul-corruption,
because of a truth.
Por una satisfacción.

You could be a Hustler and a Pimp,
the floral whipped topping
on a white creme de menthe,
the scavenging prosperity of a post war food,
mostly sweet breads
and pickled herring
in cans.

My lips are budding,
and I've never felt so young
and so old at the same time.

Cuanto vale el pan?
For the morning I am lured by a whistle,
the deepest depths of bread-making,
a labor intensive love.
Hurled into a matter that's not even my own.
But this isn't how I used to feel.

I am gaining momentum,
recibiendo una carta del jardín de mi dios.
For now being severely humbled
by the violent hail
and the malevolent grounds.
My prayers are answered.
I realize that I am the melanin
in this particular angel's cheeks.
For today,
a planting ground for Las Flores Santas.
For today,
a time-capsuled living chalice of El Vino Sagrado.

Honey Black

Sillage,
of musk blackberry pine box,
of Tabac Blond,
stream left behind a boat,
heavy and immensely masculine.
New Orleans was characterized
by a delicately composed warm rose honey.
Hot dripping promiscuous jazz
near the Basin Street Station at 501,
formerly the New Orleans terminal company.
He was known to me as at least a silver,
even though in his mind he was brass and cod.
Deformed and never at a high enough position
to wear Panama straw.
Improvisation is Honey Black.
Nola Brass Band funerals were covered in it.
Peau D'Espagne, so dry, so dusty.
Resinous, extremely striking composition to wear
and to grow up with.
Honeybee evaporated milk with charisma.
A common love for the Jelly Roll
and his Red-Hot Peppers in their navy suits.
I picked up a bar of Proctor and Gamble Ivory Soap,
because I heard the powder flakes could be used to make "homemade snow"
for jerry-built Christmas decorations.
I love Christmas, the skin scent, the rouge,
the marzipan imitations of fruits and vegetables,
and the snow.

Sillage.
Nectar of two peaches.
It is of driest smoke.
Soft brown leaves with a sensitive crinkling settle in the cafe,
where there is served Tuscany soup and Cappuccino.

Somebody is wearing something much more exotic,
and it makes me feel slightly inferior.
But I remember my inspiration was taken from a man.
A very abstract balsamic male figure,

and I feel better about myself.
Improvised flower water,
tobacco,
free of fire for the most part,
imbibed through pipe not papers.
Leather, carnation, exaggerated decant,
not for the faint of heart.
Lime blossom, vetiver, ylang-ylang.
There's a little bit left in the furs she's buried in.
It smells a little bit like blood with lemons,
offensive and rewarding,
imperial and grown up.
It mellows but doesn't change.

The hawksbill tortoise shell,
Mother of pearl lacquer with peonies,
inkwell style or snuffbox,
links the bottle to its Turkish sugar orange.
Extrait de Parfum.
Intimate, close to the body,
not to be confused with another woman.
A true perfume is served on a black velvet strip,
like a cut of meat with pears.
You need several napkins.
Warms with the skin.
It is a frame of mind in its gasoline accord,
and it is never forgotten.
I'm speechless.
How can something so pearly white be so mischievous?
I want to sit in this place where this person has been.

We both have freckles in between the breasts
and different stories of Guerlain.
Mine's a ritual, time spent alone.
Powder, sophisticated, murky,
testing the patience and keeping its gospel.

It reminds me of a dream I had.
Like Mitsouko, same year, but better.
I knew from the beginning how fun it could be.

Improvisation is Honey Black.
Ever-spreading agricultural weeds.
New Orleans speaks with its bright orange
and its box theatre accomplishment.
Louisiana steamboat,
sillage,
Alabama,
the coppery froth stream left behind its back.
The American sweet bread dulled black stage of Carnegie Hall,
3,671 seats in the auditorium,
lined with bread seed Poppies.
And the whole interior smelled of wax.
He was known to me as at least a silver,
even though in his mind he was brass and cod,
deformed,
and never at a high enough position to wear an Extrait.

He just warmed olive oil and hay in his hands
to wear on the back of his neck.
And so did I because it reminded me of him.
It is not a nicotine patch.
It is not a substitute.
It is tobacco strawberry pine box:
hazy, deformed,
with base notes from sweaty Chicago and heady Alabama,
stream left behind a boat.

I love the NOLA Obituaries,
such exquisite pieces of literature.
But mostly I love the smell of the newspapers.
Improvisation is Honey Black:
butter, leather, nausea, carnation.
Not for the faint of heart.
Vaults decorated with thousands of burnt pink flowers
in Saint Louis Cemetery II on All Saints Day.
There's a little bit left in the straw he's buried in.

A little bit like blood with lemons.
It mellows but it doesn't change.

Love

You are my cabbage and my rose.
This dandelion wine is the taste of our summers.
The fights are the citric acid,
which tempers the sting of sugar.
The curse of our love is a longtime fever in heaven.

There exists golden honeyed droplets.
Little to show for our hard work,
just the volume of the bottle.

I am sleeping alongside the idea of false dandelion,
waking consistently amongst the sewn petals of man's making.

Seeds are produced without pollination.

Lion Tooth petals are born
on hairless and leafless hollow branches.
They take life from each other's ripest forms.

You slurred "Paris" to me,
and I couldn't help but burst into drunken laughter.
There was rose oil on my lips,
and you licked it off.

To feel warm in your heart
and hot in your soul
to the point of your blood running thin,
makes all the moneyless evenings lucrative.

We do everything to keep from losing the red color,
from seeing it on our skin.
We stop heaving from loss,
hurting for the other one,
until we become like newborns again.

The possessions become less the motor response.
The liquid lets out,
and it spreads out in the rain rinsed daisy mash
of humanoid perennial blossoms.

We can just stay here,
and we can be together,
and take comfort in our sweltering life.

Feel my bright blue body,
and recognize it as your own.
I'm you.
I'm alive to make sense of the drugs you divided at birth,
the freedoms we decided we'd give each other,
before we could speak or walk.

Your orgasm is a tangent.
Mine, a departure.

My blessed pearls,
make love and keep it inside,
just like a woman does.
She aches,
just like a woman does,
and he's hungry to pick up her strewn parcels.

Sancocho

Don't hold my hand.
Don't kiss my cheek.

Know by heart my sensuality,
My friendship.
And feel me from a distance,
For distance is all there is.

I'm taking lessons.
I've decided to become a subservient novice
At a few different trades.
I'm studying The Baptism of Christ
By Piero della Francesca.

Stay over there,
While I sit over here.
Let me fix you tea without using my hands.
Sancocho, without tasting it.
It's been simmering all day long.

I'm learning how to French Kiss without any contact.
I'm learning how to be alone in my house,
While you're in the house with me.

Like an upright plant,
You gush when you are frozen.
You find comfort in familiarity
And mundane life.
You smile without being stimulated.

The human against the milk sky is abundant:
Nurturing, satisfying, decaying.

There is no neutrality without touch.
Only love and heartbreak.
Overflowing, bubbly, uncontainable love
And heartbreak.

It's decadent and disturbing.
It's rich herbed sopa con yuca y mazorca.

Feminine and masculine and raw and great.
Like the release of butterflies in Hyde Park, 1969.

Bring me back my blushing rose,
And I'll trade in the skimmed, perpetual broth
For a day longer to feel what's really there.

Twenty Five

I've spent these days trying to remember
what the saltwater felt like in my hair
during the savory arch of my last birthday.
Imagining the drying, saltish and stinging response
of the skin on the scalp.
The sunny wet walk from the boat to the dock.
I am tender at the thought of a witty and malnourished
middle life that may sprout to a proper imperial span.
Last sweaty summer,
I spent my days in the bathroom,
which was my office.
And I drank warm Mexican beer,
while I painted self-portraits
sitting on the sink.
The crowded brown glass
keeps the light from burning my skin
through the open window,
so that I may remain preserved,
planted at twenty-five,
around the forfeit of staunch and tropic flowers.

Last autumn
I stared at a gash in the wood
of a yellow doorway in a bistro.
The floor started falling away
into the water that was beneath it,
and every wall was Italian stained glass.
I slipped away too,
and I was floating.
The water seemed holy,
the beige variances of Cupid.
I could feel the ripples
and the weight of milk.
Having dreamt only last night that I was to be a mother,
I placed my hands on my belly,
and I was looking for my child.
But my womb was empty.
And I was awake.

Nevada

I.

Summer is a place of rest for winter degradation.
Red heat herds memory seeds.
Hulls, pregnant, crackle under sun dust imminent
in this desert.

My shell steeps in just boiled water
to heat my blood and give me new perspective:
violet, frothy, noteworthy,
plated with small seventies vegetable print.

My body is bigger than it was last May.
I fit into shoes tailored for women long passed.
I feel the pressure of their life weight,
humble dramatist reign,
sewn with tarnished thread into my scalloped lace.

My perfume is theirs too.
A China Ceylon balm that is European
but not too heavy in the back of the throat.

Its cinéma brings back a time of solace and late supper,
a grieving night's fire that burns to evil green,
before I can get up to dance.

II.

I think certain people, certain families,
find me pleasant and familiar,
warm and rosy in the cheeks.
They want to take me in, raise me.
They want me to linger late,
make lemon sorbet in their living room
and see my smile stay sleepy and underwhelmed.

I could inhale the sheets and wander around,
taking from stale air,
wishing for something prominent and loose.

I could marry into the family,
be someone's in-law,
have an affair with a brother.
I could drink until I fall asleep.

Sherry proves to me its sweetness,
festers in my esophagus.
It is perfect to drink when already drunk,
or with cherries in a charlotte bowl,
otherwise filled with purple Taggiasca.

Amontillado's affronted treasure.
Seventy days of rainfall,
three hundred days of sunshine.
A summer burgundy base for residual debts.

III.

There is a table in a musky old house
in an orange valley that provides support
to a glass of clouded Rhone
that I sip only when you're with me.

A black and bludgeoned berry lit room
gives way to renaissance friendship.

Having hated, having killed,
having loved more than life,
we lay in an ice-cold stream together
with our boots on.
A strange and timeless gift
that has its roots in birth and pain.

I need a secret for my heart.
A meal, a thread.
I need to touch,
and you change with vanishing time.
I like to make one feel a certain way,
change their mood.

I miss getting nervous.
I don't know when it happened,
possibly when I learned "ducky" is a part of speech.

It means to be taken care of,
like being carried away sometimes
or being kept up in the quiet morning.

Maybe it was when I learned that "dew dropper",
a lovely and nostalgic term from childhood,
refers to an unemployed man who sleeps all day.

IV.

I want to curl up in a rain drenched afternoon,
when the flowers were brought discipline,
listen to a stranger's pitter patter on the floor beyond me.

Parents' bedrooms are forbidden and mysterious.

I think of being in a music wood rose room,
a sauna with a girlfriend.

I look into someone's eyes admiringly,
and hers are gusty with lashes,
wide set and emotional.

V.

Nevada is still and never leaves.
It is ground I fall onto within the lifespan of a certain eclipse.
I feel I want to reside with you there at the edge of July.
Spend your birthday giving water to heated ground.
Treat every day like a weekend
and remember when dirty guys on holiday
remembered me from a time before,
bringing me late breakfast on a patio somewhere,
calling me jailbait to their friends before I was of age.

VI.

I am in an elevator with a fur coat on.
It rises and falls with your breath in the florescence,
and I can taste your aftersmoke.

I feel somehow reattached when I,
a young woman,
a Gen Y obsessive follower,
start to perform old woman acts.

Feeling comfortable in them,
I play out my future with old clothes,
stockings and hats.
Taking into consideration my working eye,
I put on sentimental lighting
and remember when I was twenty.

I am in Nevada with after hour documents.
My eyes are old and dry.

You're only a piece,
my after-hour heaven.
You're only a poem,
a tattoo, a dried fruit,
a sliver of moon.

VII.

When I have my babies,
I'll grip shallow pools of relic granules.
Test the waters.

You said you wanted to learn more about living,
that flowers are important:
sprigs of yellow wheat, crown of laurels,
a bite of purple specimen in the course black.

There remains my desire to kiss you
and push you into the crowded interface,

before I move to California,
before my books are published,
before my life is started.

I will see you face to face,
this last time I am with you,
in Nevada.

Muerte

A little boy awoke to fresh pastries on one mild weather morning.
The next day, to the smell of death.
Cows gutted in the field,
the air smelled clean like death.
Blood, protein, glucose,
metabolic waste.
The black bile and the phlegm.

Blood never runs clear.
A droplet tints the water of the clean puffy womb
a rosy pink

The next spring, the land is lush with nutrients.
Beautiful flowers grow.

Dahlias bloom in August.
They are tubers like potatoes.
They copyright all the names because they are so exotic.
And since the naming, I took a step into your grave,
even laid my full body into it,
and proceeded to laugh and cry at all the jokes you told me.

I woke up on the side of the road
in a wind farm
in Kansas.
The whirring of turbines,
a symbol of ever-changing life.
You were on the other side of the gargantuan machine,
and then you were whisked away into the clouds.

The congruent bedding for flowers loved the sediment
and calcium from the memory's nightcap.
Pour one out for the homies,
and you'll wake up to Begonia.

Gangsters love home cooking.
Gangsters love me.

And now I am learning the importance of remembering each birth date,
each marriage date, and each death date.

Each happy anecdote over a glass of ordinary beer,
each shower,
each skin to skin,
each turkey sandwich,
each dream for the future.

The fact that he spoke so fondly of the ocean amused me,
since he had never been to California.

The gravity is warm evening soaked,
gathering in my ankles,
waiting to perform a frothy, gratuitous pleasure.

Stagnant is a neutral mood.
No music. No flowers.
No food or sex.
Just shallow breaths and a significant month of rest.

Your eyes are milky and searching,
black and bulging from watching birds all afternoon.
Your heart, a tender oversized remnant
picked from the chalk of last year's monogamy.

Now I know I can break your heart
if I break my own in the process.
The girl is a cavity like a chicken carcass
with an apple and a quarter onion inside.

Left against the backdrop of blue air,
fermenting and lulled by the larvae.
There is a cluster of midsummer crop with an aggregate fruit structure
that is grown to discolor our mouths when we kiss.

It is a labor of love like anything can be.
Like muddling fresh cardamom
or making honey out of lard.

With Thanks

Many thanks to my friends and family, ancestors and mentors, to New Mexico my home, and to the artist, the mongrel, the hillbilly and the vagabond.

Special thanks to my husband, Kyle Thomas. When I met you, I saw you on my horizon, your back against the setting sun. And then I saw us, lit up and colored red and peach by the backdrop of a sacred earth. Thank you, Angel, for always stoking my fire and also for having the extinguisher ready when we accidentally set the world aflame.

Special thanks also to my sister, Tai. Your ineffable beauty and heart inspire me every day. To my mom and dad. Thank you for putting bread on the table, for grounding us in spirituality and love, and for showing your girls how to be creative, spirited, wild and free. And to my incredible, inspiring grandparents.

Natachee Momaday Gray is New Mexico poet and artist whose work focuses on the melding of art and myth, ancestry and nostalgia, food and prayer, glamour, frivolity, and time. She is a winner of the University of New Mexico Lena Todd Award in poetry. Her work has appeared in several publications, including the *Taos Journal of International Poetry and Art and (RE) An Ideas Journal*. Her poems have also been featured at several venues in Santa Fe and Taos, New Mexico including Teatro Paraguas, the Richard Eeds radio show, Collected Works Bookstore, and as a SOMOS reader at the Harwood Museum.

A native of Santa Fe, she has many artistic talents as a poet, hand fashioned bookmaker, fiction writer, Chanteuse, and film maker. In her uniquely creative voice, she draws on her Kiowa and Apache heritage to create compelling stories that transcend designation.

Natachee is the daughter of abstract expressionist artist and musician Darren Vigil Gray and actress/writer/film maker Jill Momaday. She is the granddaughter of Pulitzer Prize-winning author N. Scott Momaday.

www.ingramcontent.com/pod-product-compliance
Lightning Source LLC
Chambersburg PA
CBHW022125090426
42743CB00008B/1005